P9-CQK-641

On the Enjoyment of Modern Art

by

Jerrold Morris

An Explanatory Text
Illustrated by Canadian Paintings

Society for Art Publications
McClelland and Stewart Limited
Toronto/Montreal

Design: Paul Arthur & Associates Ltd. (Gerhard Doerrié)
Printed and bound: Helio Gravure Inc., Montreal

The Canadian Publishers
McClelland and Stewart Limited
25 Hollinger Road, Toronto 16

Introduction

So many books have been written about Modern Art that some explanation may be needed for adding to the flood of words on this subject. I have written Modern Art with capitals because these two words, which simply mean art recently produced, have come to imply and include all the art of the last half-century which is not naturalistic, and therefore felt by many to be obscure, frustrating, and beyond comprehension.

There is today a revival of interest in the arts, unmatched since the Renaissance. It is probably stimulated by many factors, such as increased leisure, more efficient means of communication, wider distribution of wealth (resulting in patronage on a broader base), the investment motive, and even the desire for social status. But I believe that these are only surface manifestations of a deeper and perhaps unconscious need. As we move further into a technological age, we feel in a new way the necessity of art in our lives. The products of the artists are among the last hand-made things on earth, and we have learned to value their unique and original quality. I think also that, as our knowledge of early civilizations has increased, we have come to believe that it is the things man has created which have lasting importance and that the arts are the supreme expression of the human spirit.

This essay does not imply criticism of the many excellent books that have been published, but it is specifically addressed to those who still ask the same questions despite the millions of words that have been written. Part of the problem rests in the difficulty of expounding one medium in terms of another. It may be that some writers have made their readers feel inadequate, or not members of the club, and so discouraged them. There is also the temptation for the erudite critic to turn his exposition into a work of art for its own sake, at the expense of the subject he is discussing. The artist himself is often unhelpful at the preliminary stage: if he could write or say what he wishes to express, why should he paint it? This is not to suggest that statements and letters of artists are not valuable material for study at a later stage.

Many books have been written attacking Modern Art, whose only possible purpose is to influence artists—to set them on another course. Could a similar voice in the fifteenth century, crying that art was being secularized, have held back the tide of humanism of the Renaissance? Or could it have stopped the great sweep of Baroque Art in favour of continued worship of the masters of the High Renaissance? Modern Art is a great international movement which has spread its influence to every part of the world where human expression is free. It is futile to attack it on any grounds—sociological, philosophical, or religious. The only thing to do is to study it with a view to enjoying it, always remembering that it does not displace or destroy the art of the past, which remains as our heritage: it merely adds to it.

It is also well to remember that naturalism spans a very brief period of art history. Many of the art forms we admire today were non-naturalistic: for instance, Egyptian, Assyrian, all the early art of the West such as Archaic Greek, Etruscan, and Byzantine, as well as the art of the Far East. All we can say with certainty is that new art-forms will arise in the future, and that the art of our time will eventually take its place in history.

This essay is an attempt to open a way to the enjoyment of contemporary art. It is not a scholarly work: its intention is to be persuasive, and years of research would not have made it more so. I have tried to avoid all jargon and to use words in their commonly accepted sense. There are no footnotes. Where artists' names have come naturally to mind in certain contexts, they have been used without comment. The interested reader may refer to them elsewhere.

Part One

The Approach

We might first define some of the negative attitudes which make the approach to Modern Art difficult. The first is an emotional reaction, usually accompanied by such comments as "Hideous", "Mad", "Daubs", that stems from a natural fear of the unknown and our tendency to stand on guard against the unfamiliar. Another frequently heard remark is "My child could do better." This betrays a misunderstanding of the artist's aims. For reasons which will appear later many people appraise painting by its "recognizability," linked with a quality usually called "beauty." As the Modern artist's purpose is seldom concerned with these qualities, it is as futile to measure his work by them as to try to read French with a German dictionary. Then there is the "Who's fooling whom?" attitude. This is based on the proposition that artists are spending their devoted lives for the purpose of pulling our legs.

Finally, and much more sinister, are the attempts to make political hay out of Modern Art by suggesting that it is in some way subversive or decadent. These attacks are also emotionally directed, but they deliberately seek to capitalize on popular prejudice. If the greatest task of our age is to preserve the freedom and the dignity of the individual, then the artist stands in the front ranks of democracy. Certainly many artists have expressed a strong social conscience: Goya, Courbet, some American painters of the Depression, and Picasso, to mention a few. But one has only to look at the sterile art of Hitler Germany and Soviet Russia to recognize that Modern Art is a symptom of political freedom.

In all these attitudes, which express a determination to maintain our own position against that taken by the artist, there is a suggestion of arrogance. Most of the great artists of the past have been misunderstood by their contemporaries. This does not mean that we should be prepared to accept humbly the whole vast production of Modern Art but a little humility will help.

The next requirement is a willingness to try to discover the artist's aims. If we do not know what he is attempting to do, we cannot judge the results.

We must also be prepared to gain looking experience, until we are thoroughly familiar with the idiom of painting. This is the only way to develop critical faculties; there is no short cut. Whatever, of a philosophical nature, an artist puts into a picture, a visual image must result, which is subject to criticism by aesthetic standards. Although time will in any case separate the good from the bad, it is the job of the expert and the critic to hasten the process. However, while the capacity to judge can only be acquired by application, all of us can enjoy modern paintings if we will look at them as fresh experiences. If we approach them in a receptive spirit, we can certainly receive some part of their message without any specialized study. We cannot influence the mode of expression of our artists, nor should we try to. But while granting them this freedom, we retain the right to accept or reject their creations. If we reject them without any attempt at understanding, we ourselves will be the only losers.

An artist is a person of unusual sensibility, who is charged or excited by visual impressions or concepts. Eventually he will discharge these impressions in works of art, which might be described as communications. The acuteness of his sensibility, the depth of his humanity, his skill in handling his medium—all these contribute to his stature. If we can receive his message, we shall be enriched by the experience. It will help us to shed our indifference and achieve an added awareness of the nature of matter, the quality of things, the character of man, and the endless fascination of images. Bernard Berenson called this "life enhancement."

The Artist in Society

The position of the artist in society has changed radically during the last hundred years. In the Middle Ages artists ranked as craftsmen and were organized into guilds, such as the Guild of St. Luke, which ensured thorough training under the apprenticeship system. Artists attached to a court were expected to apply themselves not only as portrait painters but in the production of medals, coins, effigies, and miniatures, as well as decorations for fêtes, ceremonies, plays, and receptions. Their standing was no higher than that of a builder or engineer.

For hundreds of years the Church was the greatest patron of the arts but maintained a rigid control over the artist's work, specifying subject matter to the last detail. These details were often determined by written contract, and an artist could even be hailed before the Inquisition to explain any unusual treatment of a religious subject—as occurred in the case of Veronese. Within this framework of patronage, however, artists seem to have worked generally without frustration and the guild system they found to their advantage. At their own request a charter was granted to the Company of Painter-Stainers in 1575 by Queen Elizabeth of England, to safeguard the proper training of craftsmen.

In carrying out the functions necessary to society, artists were content with their status as craftsmen. Patronage involved controls, but artists of great talent were able to transcend restrictions on their freedom. It was not until the eighteenth century that Reynolds deliberately set out to raise the social standing of painters, although artists before his time, such as Raphael, Titian, and Rubens had gained immense personal prestige, and not until the nineteenth century that the idea of the artist as craftsman gave way to the romantic concept of the artist as genius.

But by this time artists were becoming less and less indispensable to their fellow men. As technology advanced, particularly in printing and photography, the artist was stripped of his functions as illustrator, propagandist, decorator and designer. Soon only the "fine arts" were left as his province.

Today we need not make a single demand of the artist: he is now a creative source which we approach only of our own free will. And yet, working in what many call his ivory tower, he has by his independent work contributed far more than most of us realize to our physical surroundings. Architecture, industrial design, advertising, packaging and textiles have all been directly influenced by artists, who have created the visual pattern of our time. We have become familiar with this pattern and feel it to be appropriate, without necessarily making any contact with the artist himself. However, many people are coming to realize the rewards that direct experience with the artist can bring. The artist has built no ivory tower: on the contrary he is eager to find once again an accepted place in society and, whenever he has been given the opportunity, he has proved that he can make a rich contribution. The Vence Chapel, Matisse's last great achievement, is an example of what can be accomplished by putting the artist back to work. Others will come to mind in the fields of book illustration, stage design, tapestry, stained glass, sculpture, and mural painting.

Fashions of Seeing
One of the stumbling-blocks in the path towards the acceptance of Modern Art lies in the manner of looking at it; for there are fashions of seeing. The fact that our vision is subjective is recognized by such phrases as "the scales fell from his eyes," or the Biblical reference to the healed blind man who saw "men as trees walking." This conditioning of the retinal image by the brain is controlled by the climate of the period: its social structure, religious beliefs, philosophy, and state of knowledge. We are all subject to it, but the creative artist has always struggled against it, in order to make a statement valid for his own time.

Consider our reactions to dress. If we look at a representation of any of the more extravagant fashions of the past—for example, a man dressed in the seventeenth century manner with all its laces, frills and furbelows—we are not particularly struck by its remoteness from present day wear. We may be amused or curious about dressing problems if we stop to think about them, but we are more likely to accept the style without thought, because it is sanctioned by our knowledge of history. But looking at a fashion plate of only twenty years ago, we find the styles ridiculous, ugly and entirely unsuitable, because we are looking at them with eyes conditioned by today's fashions. Our sense of what is proper in dress changes rapidly because we are accustomed to the idea that fashions change rapidly. The same applies to car models. If on the other hand we have become used to looking at some familiar group of objects, the style of which has remained static over long periods, we tend to be shocked at any radical innovation. Our attitude to the visual arts is an example of this kind of cumulative conservatism of vision. Byzantine, Egyptian and Chinese art-forms changed little in a thousand years. In the West, for six hundred years, artists laboured to make their paintings more and more naturalistic, so that people came to equate excellence in a painting with accuracy of rendering.

It is for this reason that there is so much misunderstanding of contemporary art. Whereas the artist today is largely concerned with abstract motives, most of his public is looking at his work with eyes conditioned by Renaissance seeing. For the artist a great gulf is fixed between the art of today and that of the Renaissance—a gulf set in the 1870's when the French Impressionists exhibited together. To understand the nature of this gulf and how it opened up, we shall have to survey briefly the progress of Western painting up to that time.

Byzantine

During the Middle Ages all thinking was coloured by religion. Men believed that their time on earth was but a brief sojourn before their final fate in Heaven or Hell: they tended to disregard the physical world. St. Anselm said that it was dangerous to sit in a garden, because its beauty might beguile the senses. The art of Byzantium, which reached the height of its Early period before the Iconoclastic Controversy over image worship (726-867 A.D.) and influenced the whole of Europe throughout most of the Middle Ages, was non-naturalistic. Essentially abstract and two-dimensional, it depicted no landscape. By means of a rigidly symbolical formula it sought to present the awesomeness of the Trinity, the hierarchy of the Saints, and the Biblical story.

Gothic

With the gradual break-up of the feudal system and the humanizing of religion by the teaching of St. Francis in the thirteenth century, man's interest turned increasingly to the physical world. Gothic Art, which reflected this change, was still highly stylized but more naturalistic in intention. Rigid forms were loosened into elongated soft curves; gold backgrounds began to be replaced by conventions for landscape. Above all, a more tender and passionate spirit was evident in the later Middle Ages. Religious devotion became centred on Mary, the Mother of Jesus.

Renaissance

The Renaissance has been defined as the transitional period between the mediaeval and modern ages. In its early stages the new and the old styles flourished side by side, the new spirit finding its first outlet in Italy in the fourteenth century. To the developing naturalism of Gothic art the Renaissance added humanism, the cult of the individual and with it hero worship, the search for a form of beauty related to the classic art of Greece and Rome, and the enjoyment of the temporal world. It was a time of ferment, exploration and experiment, out of which grew modern civilization.

Artists began to search for a means of representing things in their material reality. They studied linear and aerial perspective, anatomy and the mechanics of the human body in motion. The pure colours of the Gothic style were modified, as light and shade were increasingly used to define forms. Secular subjects, drawn from classical mythology, became common and the individual portrait returned to popularity for the first time since the Roman age.

It is interesting at this point to look back to the Paleolithic cave painters, who were able to translate their immediate perceptions so vividly. Centuries were to elapse before man achieved an equal facility in rendering animals in movement. Why? It certainly cannot be that Paleolithic man was endowed with any superior ability. It can only be that he was seeing with the "innocent eye," which later the Impressionists tried to cultivate: that is an eye uninhibited by styles or conventions of recording images.

The Renaissance artist's vision, subject as it was to the stylistic forms of Byzantine and Gothic art, could not make the leap to naturalism without a conscious struggle. The whole of the fifteenth century was taken up with experimentation towards naturalistic representation. The artist could not set down what he saw with the untrammelled vision of the hunters who left their drawings on the walls of the Lascaux caves; he had to laboriously re-learn to see. He had to dissect bodies, invent perspective, and then struggle to make his creatures move. When one looks at a painting by Signorelli, for instance, one can sense the artist's intense effort to make the muscles perform.

All important art movements have their periods of development, fulfilment and decline. The youthful struggle of the first half of the fifteenth century reached its fruition at its close with Da Vinci, Raphael, Michelangelo, and Titian.

This century saw a great advance in the technique of painting, during which the more refractory media of tempera and fresco gave way to the general practice of painting in oils. At the same time the elaborate processes of drawing and methodical underpainting to build up a work developed into a more painterly handling. Titian was able to work for his final effect at once, and the technique has not changed since, except by the introduction of more quickly drying paints.

The Eclectics

Many artists of the sixteenth century felt that the great ones had preceded them and paid homage to them by selecting for imitation those qualities of the Renaissance masters they admired and seeking to combine them into an ideal form. Tintoretto's reported desire to rival the colour of Titian and the drawing of Michelangelo is an example of the method. Inevitably this attempt to revive or preserve the outward form without the inner content that informed it reduced the grand to the grandiose and resulted in extravagant mannerism.

Much of the self-consciousness may have been fostered by the formation of academies, which from the sixteenth century onwards became influential and partisan. Under the apprenticeship system the artist had learned the techniques of his trade and then gone forth to develop his own style based on that of his master. The academies, however, by deliberately selecting styles from the past for emulation, tended to induce conformity in their search for an ideal.

Baroque

The seventeenth century saw the birth of a great new style, which swept the Western world like a breath of fresh air. Once again, the social climate had produced a vigorous response in artists. The main force of the Baroque style paralleled the emotional appeal of the counter-reformation. The Church now sought to persuade where formerly it had been authoritative. Church art in the seventeenth century was emotional in content, with martyrdoms, ecstasies and ascensions crowding the canvas. And the Baroque style was theatrical and turbulent, to accommodate its subjects. Compositions swirled and movement was extravagant. Another phase of Baroque art reflected in a different way the breakdown of the monolithic authority of the Church: this was an increasing trend to realism.

It is easy to imagine that Ribera's saints were modelled on beggars, and the brothers Le Nain paid homage to the dignity of labour in their grave paintings of French peasants. In Holland, which had recently been freed from the Roman Catholic yoke of Spain, art became more and more secular. The merchants and middle classes wished to see themselves and their surroundings portrayed, and the great period of Dutch art depicts the life of the burgher, the lowlife of the peasant and soldier, home interiors and still lifes and the landscape of the country.

Roccoco

The vitality of the Baroque dissipated itself in the exuberance of the Roccoco, the style of the eighteenth century. This century, which is often called the Age of Enlightenment, saw the rise to power and wealth of the middle classes and ended in the liberal upheavals of the French and American revolutions. If the Baroque was dramatic, eighteenth century art had a lightness of touch that often bordered on the frivolous. The Roccoco style is exemplified in the early works of Goya, in the revival of Venetian painting (particularly with Tiepolo), and in England with the airy quality of Gainsborough and the "fancy" pictures of Reynolds. But above all it had its flowering in France. There the arbiters of taste were women and their influence can be seen in the works of Watteau, Fragonard and Boucher. Towards the end of the century the flamboyance of the Roccoco was checked by the Neoclassical style, which looked back to Greece and Rome. The nobility of David echoed Napoleonic sentiments and in England the somewhat stilted efforts of Benjamin West, President of the Royal Academy from 1792 to 1820, were on the same rhetorical plane.

The Academies

In this brief survey we have seen that the history of Western painting consists of a sequence of more or less coherent styles—Byzantine, Gothic, Renaissance, Baroque and Roccoco—although this progression has been over-simplified for the purpose of clarity. The nineteenth century produced no such universal style, but rather a series of revolts against academic and official art. We should therefore examine what the academies had come to stand for.

The academies of England and France were both founded under government sanction. From its beginning in the eighteenth century, under the dominance of Reynolds, the Royal Academy of England proposed an ideal compounded of the art of Greece, Rome and such Renaissance artists as Raphael, diluted by an excessive admiration for the sixteenth century eclectics: for example, Guido Reni and the Carracci. Painters such as Ostade and Teniers, who drew their subjects from everyday life, were thought to be the height of vulgarity. Indeed, "history painting"—that is the use of historical, mythological or literary subjects in which human sentiments could be expressed and nature idealized—was held to be the only thing worthy of treatment by artists.

Landscape painting was considered an inferior *genre* and such a fine painter as Richard Wilson found little or no patronage. Even as late as 1829, when Constable was finally elected R.A., Lawrence told him that he was fortunate in being chosen, as there were historical painters of great merit on the list of Associates.

By the nineteenth century academic painting had degenerated into the naturalistic rendering of idealized sentiment or, more usually, sentimentality. Stendhal wrote of the artist that "He has to have a soul." He also said, "It is in an ardent and accurate portrayal of the human heart, then, that the nineteenth century will differ from all that had gone before." The more mawkish it all became, the more the public loved it; until such subjects as "The Soldier's Farewell to his Horse" appeared among the list of popular favourites. According to Henry James, "The worst horror was the acres of varnish."

Perhaps they were all taking themselves too seriously. James Johnson Sweeney has written: "For all art is essentially play—as full living is a game to be enjoyed. This is probably the basic explanation of those frail or arid reaches which occasionally appear in the history of art ... usually in the afternoon of a period: the failure of art to refresh itself in those times in play. When a culture begins to regard play as something not quite respectable, that culture is already facing sterility."

Of course there had always been rebels who had gone their own way—Blake and Goya, for instance—and fortunately Reynolds himself fell wide in his performance of the ideal he set his pupils. But it was this degeneration of the Renaissance vision that determined the popular concept of beauty—something ideal, something of sentiment, something even pretty. There is, however, a biting edge to beauty that places it alongside truth, and the significance of the nineteenth century revolts is the attempt of artists to restore this edge.

Romantics and Realists

The first challenge to academic art came with the Romantic movement of the nineteenth century. The art of Géricault and Delacroix was not only a protest against entrenched authority but also introduced romantic subject-matter—as in the North African paintings of Delacroix. In romantic painting there is an element of fiction and an emphasis on the fabulous and the sublime. In England Turner's approach to landscape was romantic and in North America the advance of the frontier was treated romantically by the Hudson River School of painters.

Hard on the heels of the Romantics came the Realists, headed by Courbet and Daumier; indeed the two movements were currents flowing together and often hard to separate.

We should here distinguish between the sense in which the words naturalism and realism are used in this essay.

Naturalism is the attempt to render a scene as it appears on the retina of the eye—in other words the intention is photographic. This motive was once a creative one, because what the artists wanted to express demanded a naturalistic form. The Franciscan concept could not be presented in Byzantine style, nor could the humanism of the Renaissance. The steps taken by artists to master the techniques of naturalistic rendering were exciting discoveries involving the creative process.

Realism, on the other hand, is a concept rather than a technique, and may be thought of as the opposite of the ideal. We have already noticed the tendency of some Baroque painters towards realism. It constantly recurs in northern painting. One has only to compare an altar-piece by Memling, for instance, with one by any of his Italian contemporaries to recognize the realism of the Flemish painter. We also find it in much seventeenth century Dutch painting—for example, the low-life pictures of Ostade or Brouwer.

Courbet and Daumier were Realists in the sense that their subjects were taken from everyday life and were deliberately anti-ideal, anti-academic. The same down-to-earth quality, with romantic overtones, can be found in the treatment of peasant subjects by Millet and Van Gogh.

By the middle of the century a group of landscape painters known as the Barbizon School had established itself near the Forest of Fontainebleau. Their approach, inspired by Constable, was naturalistic and contrary to the accepted classical canons. Among them were Corot, Rousseau, and Daubigny, the last of whom painted out-of-doors with Monet, and therefore directly influenced the Impressionists.

Impressionism

We have now reached the gulf we mentioned earlier that lies between the art of the Renaissance and Modern Art. First let us examine what Impressionism was. If we think of "impression" as being momentary superficial recognition, we can translate this, in terms of painting, into the fixing of the fugitive moment.

By this definition we shall find impressionism where the light steals across a silk in Velasquez, the heir to the Venetians; in the misty vistas of a landscape backdrop to one of Watteau's *fêtes galantes,* with their sad sense of the frailty of human life; in the flash of light where a gondolier dips his paddle in a Guardi canal; in the shimmering brushwork of a Goya portrait which seeks the very presence of the sitter; in the intense concentration of Constable before the most fleeting effects of nature; in the atmospheric symphonies of Turner.

The French Impressionists of the late nineteenth century were aware of all these artists through their studies in the Louvre. But in particular they regarded the work of men of their own century—Courbet and Delacroix, for instance—and their discoveries followed logically the fresh approach to landscape painting of Boudin, Jongkind, and the members of the Barbizon School.

French Impressionists

In the full development of their style the French Impressionists were able to declare a formula. "Light is the most important subject matter in my paintings," said Monet, and in their search for light they abandoned formal structure. The flickering brushwork of Titian's late paintings now reached its ultimate and became an established technique, involving also the analysis of light by splitting it into the colours of the spectrum. The scientific climate of the time made its contribution, as did the invention of the camera.

In his memoirs Antonin Proust quotes Manet as saying, "That's something that's not sufficiently understood today; one doesn't just paint a landscape, or a marine, or a figure study, but the impression of a moment in time."

When we look at the works of the Impressionists today, it is hard to believe that they called down upon themselves the most savage abuse. Such was the public reception of this gay and gallant attempt to present a world aglitter with light and love of life, that the painters nearly starved. Their work is now accepted universally, while our own *avant-garde* attracts a more cautious scorn.

Here again we encounter the phenomenon of fashions of seeing. At the end of the nineteenth century most people still saw landscape through the eyes of the "gravy school" of academic painters that aped the Dutch artists of the seventeenth century. The bright clean colours of the Impressionists were felt to be an outrage to the senses. Now, however, the adjustment has been made and the rainbow palette is accepted without offence.

Impressionism as such did not survive long, but its effects were lasting. In their rejection of local colour and their experimental approach to rendering of light, these artists freed colour from all reference to the object and to this extent all subsequent art movements have been in their debt.

17

Although the Impressionists were actually struggling to portray nature more accurately than ever before, their technique had other implications. When, for vibrant effect, they placed their touches of red and green, or violet and orange (colours which are not to be found in this pure form in nature) side by side, they suggested to other artists the possibility of using colour in an arbitrary manner. The touches of the Impressionists became the hatchings in pure colour that Van Gogh used for expressive purposes, and the flat colour areas of Matisse, the Fauves and the German Expressionists.

The reaction against the formlessness of Impressionism led, through the experiments of Cezanne and Seurat, to the exploration of form in Cubism. Here were the two vital components of Modern Art—arbitrary colour and free form—and, by implication, the pre-eminence of the picture itself, freed of naturalistic reference to subject matter. It was not long before both these paths, the expressive and the formal, led to non-objective painting, the expressive through Kandinsky and the formal through Cubism.

Objective is used here to denote any painting in which recognizable subject matter is retained; non-objective to denote paintings in which no subject matter appears.

The Gulf

Beyond this point there is no need to pursue the historical method. The various movements by which Modern Art developed after Impressionism have been amply documented in many excellently illustrated books. The remainder of the first section of this essay will be devoted to a discussion of Modern Art in general terms; in the second section we shall deal specifically with some of its more important manifestations. But at this climactic moment we should pause for a while to recapitulate.

From the Gothic age onwards the whole trend of Western art was towards increasing naturalism. But we should not make the mistake of believing that this progression was in fact progress. It is safe to assume that man in all periods is equipped with equal talent and that he will bring this talent to bear with equal force on the environment in which he lives. Creative artists do not become more talented from century to century; they merely work in different states of society. The measure and limit is always the genius of the individual. We find great painters in all periods, and it is completely unrewarding to attempt to grade them.

One of the fallacies of the academic doctrine of the nineteenth century was the proposition that, as the techniques at the disposal of artists improved, paintings became better and better. The test of an academic painting was "How lifelike is it?" and this test is still applied by a great many people. By this standard Gothic art was thought to be untutored and the works of primitive societies were looked upon as curiosities suitable only for inclusion in ethnological museums. It should never be forgotten that man is the measure of all things and that it is wholly possible for a Benin carver to be as great an artist as any sculptor who has ever lived.

Modern Art was born of a revolt against the sterile naturalism of the academies, when artists began the search for a new truth that would be valid for their own medium. From the camera they had learned a new way to record "the exact instant," but they refused to compete with it as an instrument to register appearances. They knew that the Old Masters did not have naturalism as a primary objective, and they carefully examined their works in the museums to discover what had been lost. They found that the great painters of the past had always been concerned with formal considerations as a means to expressiveness: that the demands of the picture itself had always been paramount.

New Concepts

We have shown that art is an expression of the climate of a particular time—its religion, social organization, knowledge and philosophy. As Bernard Shaw wrote, "What I say today, everybody will say tomorrow, though they will not remember who put it into their heads. Indeed, they will be right; for I never remember who puts things into my head: it is the Zeitgeist." We should now try to determine in what manner Modern Art is an expression of our age. One can say, "The world is mad; Modern Art is a manifestation of a disturbed age," but this negative way of shrugging off the art of our time as an aberration will not do: it is simply not the truth.

There are probably three factors which have most affected the development of twentieth century art.

The first is the new concept of matter. The physics taught in the nineteenth century proposed that the smallest particle, the atom, was indivisible—a kind of minute billiard ball— and I suppose that matter was conceived of as being composed of tightly packed miniature billiard balls. But atomic physics has disposed of this idea of the virtual impenetrability of matter: we now think of it as being in a constant state of flux, electrons and all the other particles shooting through areas of space, and even of matter as being interchangeable with energy. This fundamental change in concept is reflected in Modern Art. One has only to look at a canvas by Jackson Pollock to sense this whirl of particles. This is not to say that artists have deliberately set out to paint pictures of fission, but they can now take liberties with the material world which would have been inconceivable to the Renaissance painter.

The second great influence has been psychiatry and the exploration of the sub-conscious. The revelation that below the level of consciousness there are unrealized impulses which control our behaviour and affect our personality has assumed enormous importance for our society. Artists were immediately intrigued by this field and began to explore the possibilities of metaphysical expression and surrealist painting, in which dreams were given figuration and the sub-conscious plumbed for images. Although the use of surrealist subject matter was confined to comparatively few artists, the method of allowing the sub-conscious to dictate the form was very common. In fact a large proportion of today's painting is performed on the level of intuition controlled by intelligence. Picasso said, ". . . to search means nothing in painting, to find is the thing."

In an age in which physicists uncover more and more imponderables and postulate laws of probability, and man stands at the threshold of space, is it not understandable that the artist should also want to plumb the mysteries, to extend the frontiers of human experience, and should no longer be interested in representing mundane subjects?

The third factor is one of communication. Part of an artist's experience is his acquaintance with other art, and here the enormous diversity of his knowledge has greatly affected the modern artist. Whereas a Sienese of the fifteenth century would have to wait for a Florentine to pass through his town before he could learn anything of the flowering of Renaissance art, an artist anywhere in the world today is constantly aware not only of all contemporary art-forms but of all the known art of the past. Their discovery of Japanese prints influenced the Impressionists and Van Gogh. Negro sculpture influenced the Cubists. Pre-Columbian art influenced Henry Moore.

It is not only in the present day that such influences are operative; art has always fed on art. Consider the relationship between the painters in these three groups. Rubens—Watteau—Renoir, Titian—Delacroix—Van Gogh, Velasquez—Goya—Manet. One could construct many such bridges over the centuries. Now, however, the art of all times is within the scope of every painter's vision.

The Autonomy of the Picture
The key to the understanding of Modern Art is acceptance of the autonomy of the picture. This means that every consideration must be subordinated to the requirements of the picture itself, to the form and expression of the artist's statement.

The total organization of a work of art (aside from subject matter) is usually termed its "form," and it is the source of the aesthetic pleasure we get from contemplating it. "Remember," Maurice Denis wrote in his *Theories* of 1890, "that a painting, before being a war horse, a nude woman or some sort of anecdote, is essentially a flat surface covered with colours assembled in a certain order."

There has been much investigation, speculation and theorizing on the subject of aesthetics, which might be defined as the science of perception. It will suffice here to say that the aesthetic pleasure we get from a work of art is akin to the impression we receive from watching the "form" of a fine athlete. It is dependent on the success with which the artist has conveyed his message in terms of his medium. When the artist abuses his medium, for instance by torturing paint into foliage to induce the viewer to forget that it is above all paint, or by obliterating the canvas surface with cunning effects which become an end in themselves any satisfaction we may derive from the result must be other than aesthetic.

To clarify the point, we might compare painting with music. Beethoven's Pastoral Symphony is not an agglomeration of transcribed country sounds; it is a formal expression of human experience in notes. Similarly, Cezanne's "*Mont St. Victoire*" is not a literal rendering of a landscape; it is a formal expression of human experience in paint.

Poetry is tied to the spoken word, the visual arts to the perceptible world; only music is free. The modern artist has tried to cast out all the non-aesthetic content which had cluttered up and debased the art of painting and has yearned increasingly towards the pure abstract form of music.

However objective the content of the work, he has tried to respect his medium. At his most successful he has combined content with "form" into a homogeneous statement; it is then that we get the greatest aesthetic pleasure from contemplating his work. This is true of the great art of all periods and races.

All art forms have declined when their clear purpose and integrity have been lost. It was the final degeneration of Renaissance art into nineteenth century naturalism against which the modern artist revolted. In any discussion of changing art forms the word revolt often occurs. But these movements were not only struggles against the shackles of the past; they were positive responses to the challenge of the present. Art, in constantly renewing itself, looks forward rather than backward. André Gide wrote, "For the true artist it is no longer a matter of finding support in the art that preceded him in order to go further, but rather changing the aim of art, of inventing a new direction for his effort."

"The kind of good which art pursues", wrote Thomas Aquinas, "is not the good of the human will or appetite, but the good of the very works done or artifacts." When we speak of the autonomy of the picture, we are speaking of "the good of the very works done." In the simplest terms, a painting is an object made by an artist out of some kind of paint on a ground, and his only concern is that the work should be good. Any other consideration is determined by convention.

In this rigorous search for the "good" the true artist practices morality and, to the extent that his work draws us beyond our own selfish confines, it may be regarded as religious in character. The idea of the artist as a moral being may not be too familiar, because we confuse social with moral standards. Perhaps we prefer the bohemian idea, anyway. Artists have certainly often been anti-social, but so have hermits. The heroic life of Monet, the dedication of Van Gogh, the destruction of their own works by Rouault, Miro and others are examples of moral integrity.

The integrity of the artist, however, is reflected above all in the work. Sir Herbert Read wrote, ". . . the morality is implicit in the art, in the form and the style of it, finally in the impalpable tone of it." And D. H. Lawrence, "The essential function of art is moral. But a passionate, implicit morality, not didactic. A morality which changes the blood, rather than the mind."

Before discussing content in Modern Art we should further explore the abstract components of the picture itself: line, colour and spatial organization.

Line and Colour

The Greeks observed that certain proportions produced a sense of harmony. This enabled them to formulate the Golden Rule Section, which is still in use today. Artists have always been aware of such formal considerations.

As Delacroix put it: "There exists an impression which results from certain arrangements of colours, lights and shadows, etc. This is what might be called the music of a picture." Delacroix is here referring to what we have called "form"—that evocative organization of the picture which is not dependent on content. The phrase "music of the picture" is interesting in its suggestion of the parallel we have indicated between modern painting and the abstract quality of music.

Gauguin in a letter to Schuffenecker in 1885 wrote, "Some lines are noble, some deceptive, etc. A straight line suggests the infinite, a curved line suggests creation . . . Colours are still more explanatory . . . because of their impact on the eyesight. Certain lines are noble, others vulgar; certain harmonies are peaceful, others are comforting, others are exciting in their audacity."

Van Gogh, writing to his brother, Theo, said, "I exaggerate the fairness of the hair; I come even to orange tones, chromes and pale lemon-yellow. Beyond the head, instead of painting the ordinary wall of the mean room, I paint infinity, a plain background of the richest, intensest blue that I can contrive, and by this simple combination of the bright head against the rich blue background I get a mysterious effect, like a star in the depths of an azure sky."

All these statements recognize the fact that painting is not dependent on literary references for communication—it has its own language. Indeed an artist cannot place a vertical stroke of black paint on a virgin canvas without making some kind of statement, and this statement will be totally different if his brush stroke is horizontal and green.

Undoubtedly our sense of form (our aesthetic sense) derives form the form we find in nature. Is it not by the distortion of this form that the artist achieves his personal expression; and by a general departure from it that period styles are created?

Space

Space has been interpreted in many ways in different periods. Byzantine art was two-dimensional and indicated space by abstract means. For instance, the great proscenium arch, painted a flat blue with stars scattered over it, was read by the viewer as the awesome heavens. Gothic art suggested space by landscape symbols, until Giotto enlarged it by the placement of his monumental figures. With Uccello's first use of mathematical perspective in the early fifteenth century, space began to be created by illusive means. To these Masaccio and Piero della Francesca added aerial perspective by adjusting tonal values. Later the picture was arranged like the flats of a stage set and the eye was carried from one set to another by compositional devices. The Baroque artist advanced space forward beyond the picture plane towards the viewer. The nineteenth century, with its romantic concept of infinity, specialized in misty blue backgrounds which carried the eye into infinite distance and produced an almost hypnotic sense of yearning. (One still hears people say of a painting, "It's got a lot of distance.")

The modern artist (unless he uses naturalism for purposes that will be discussed in Part 2) uses space as an integral part of his picture; he does not seek to hide the canvas with an illusive image but refers all his planes to the picture surface. The sense of space is created by the organization of colour and by composition. Planes and lines are arranged in such a way as to produce a picture space.

Incidentally, Eastern art also rejected the illusive means. In both Chinese and Persian painting, for instance, perspective was suggested by placing those objects farthest from the viewer at the top of the picture, and working downwards towards the foreground.

Then there is the question of our reaction to painting which, although conveyed through the eyes, is in fact muscular. Berenson in his book, "The Florentine Painters," published in 1896, first formulated the theory of "tactile values"—that is to say, muscular responses to pictures. He was referring to our physical realization of the palpable three-dimensionality and space as we contemplate certain paintings of the Renaissance. This same physical participation can be felt when we look at many modern paintings, particularly large non-objective works in which the human scale is involved.

Content
The content of works of art has for the most part been determined by patronage. As we have already seen, during the Middle Ages the Church specified subject matter down to the last detail. For the first time finished paintings were offered on the market in Holland in the seventeenth century to find their own purchasers. This meant that if an artist expected to be successful he had to paint pictures likely to be in demand. Another result of this was specialization, one artist concentrating on still-lifes, another on interiors, and so on. By the nineteenth century private patronage had declined to the point where the artist was dependent on the market to live.

When the Impressionists started to paint pictures that nobody wanted at any price, a new situation developed. For several decades, as new movements followed each other, there were few patrons and practically no market, and to this extent the artists were freed of any necessity to consider the requirements of possible buyers. They drew together in groups and movements, arranged exhibitions, issued manifestos, and pursued their own search for new means of expression. This same exclusiveness, in the sense of a disregard for public demand, has continued to the present day. The contemporary artist paints to fulfill his own capabilities and not for a particular market.

James Johnson Sweeney in his lecture, "Art before Noon," said, ". . . the present day artist frankly admits that the world he is creating in his artistic medium—paint on canvas, stone, wood, metal—is essentially and inescapably out of his inner self; whereas his mid-nineteenth century predecessors in great part still believed in the possibility of a scientific record of the outside world and that communication in painting and sculpture depended on the familiar legibility of convention, or on the scientific validity of such records. To the present day artist a painting or sculpture is primarily and predominantly interesting for its own sake; and only minimally for its associations."

This situation is unprecedented in art history and has important implications. Faced with a blank canvas and with no patron at his shoulder to call the tune, the artist is free to express himself in any manner he wishes. But this freedom is very demanding, because it is without the imposed disciplines that support the feeble. Only the truly creative can find the necessary self-discipline to face that blank canvas with courage. Lesser men will cover it with the products of their own frustration or with meaningless works of the new academy.

As has been stated earlier, the schools, by setting up certain styles for emulation, tended to induce conformity and adherence to formulae. Thus, the word "academic" is used in the general sense of "appertaining to the academies," but it may also be applied to empty derivative work of any period. A great deal of the non-objective art produced today is academic in the latter sense. There have always been popularizers of creative art—for instance Schreyer's borrowing of Delacroix's North African themes and Le Sidaner's watering-down of Impressionism. Today many artists, who have absolutely nothing to say, adopt the idioms of Modern Art.

To quote again from Sweeney's lecture, "Art before Noon": "One of the first requirements for an artist is that he be a pioneer, an explorer of fresh fields of expression . . . An artist's creative value is measured by the freshness and individuality of the statements he makes, in keeping with the grammar of the medium in which he has chosen to express himself."

When I speak of an artist's responsibility constantly to cultivate some fresh corner of the field of expression, it is in the spirit of Stravinsky's famous phrase that describes the true artist as "always looking for a cool place on the pillow." The lazy artist is satisfied with the place he finds his head on; and the academician merely presses his head into even warmer, more familiar depths. As Jean Cocteau has said, "The artist must always take care when once a work has fallen from the tree, not to shake the tree to bring down others of the same kind."

The form of a work may vary from the violently expressive to a withdrawn considered classicism, the content from naturalistic to non-objective, but the concept must come from within the artist himself. He has his own experience as a sensitive human being, his delight in the visual world, the fertility of his imagination and, above all, his capacity to tap sources of power beyond himself. Art is in this respect akin to religious experience in that the creative artist is able to transcend his own conscious capabilities by seeking what used to be called "inspiration." Actually the idea of the artist as a creature of supercharged emotions who pours these emotions forth onto canvas in a state of inspiration is hardly accurate. Most paintings are begun quite cold-bloodedly and any emotion involved is engendered during the process of the work, when the artist will be carried "beyond himself." As Gide expressed it, ". . . pay attention only to the form; the emotion will come spontaneously to inhabit it." Rodin put this in another way: "One must never try to express an idea by form. Make your form, make something, and the idea will come." It is this contact with something greater than himself which makes the creative artist a dedicated person and keeps him absorbed with his work whether or not it receives recognition.

The content of the work, then, may concern the world of perception, or the sphere of human experience and emotion; or it may be imaginative and derived from all levels of consciousness. The method of communication may be direct and naturalistic, or abstract in degrees varying from minor distortion to the completely non-objective.

Signs and symbols may be used to convey meaning. From earliest times symbols have been used in religious and magic rites, the sun perhaps being the earliest. In many cases the symbol was regarded as the incarnation of the spirit represented and was itself worshipped. The Cross provides a good example of how a simple sign can become a powerful evocative image. The use of the skull in *"momento mori"* paintings is another example. Throughout art history signs, or conventions, as they are usually termed, have been used—conventions for stars, for clouds, for landscape, for water. Gainsborough's hook shapes are conventions for leaves, Canaletto's wavesigns represent water. The modern artist may also use signs: even an arrow will indicate movement in a certain direction. Other artists have gone further. Mathieu, for instance, states that the artist in the past, given an object, invented a sign for it; whereas now he may make a sign which can itself become viable. "Instead of the reduction of the Cosmos to Man, the work of art becomes an opening onto the Cosmos." In other words, the sign may suggest meanings beyond normal human experience.

Meaning may also be conveyed metaphorically, as in the case of Tamayo's dogs, which suggest the brutality of war, or Marino Marini's horse and rider, which comment on the state of man. This kind of content is discussed further under the heading "metaphysical painting" in Part 2.

This analysis of the form and content of Modern Art suggests that we may expect to find objective art in which naturalism has given place to varying degrees of abstraction and distortion for expressive and formal purposes—that is for the sake of the inherent design of the picture—or non-objective art in which we will find not a blue dress against a yellow chair, but blue against yellow; not atmospheric space, but picture space;

not meaning, but shades of meaning; not the obvious, but mystery; not the literal, but the evocative and the equivocal. Tolstoy wrote, "The aim of art is not to resolve a question irrefutably, but to compel one to love life in all its manifestations."

Technique

In addition to the responses we feel to colour and line, there is the sensuous quality of pigment itself. When we talk of an artist's work as being "painterly," we are acknowledging his skill in the handling of his medium. For centuries it was found that bristles mounted on a wooden handle provided the best tool for the manipulation of paint. Nowadays we are always hearing of some clown who rides a bicycle over a canvas or drags his girl friend across it. These stories are naturally a great comfort to the detractors of Modern Art, but there is no reason why an artist should not use any tool—palette knife, squeegee, or even his hands—if the work demands it. It is well known that Pollock laid his canvas on the floor and dripped paint on it from a can. Why not, if the works justified the method? As a matter of fact, the results he achieved could not have been attained in any other way.

The Approach

Art must be approached in a friendly and receptive spirit, with suitable humility. We must not bring to a picture preconceived ideas or demands of our own which may inhibit our contact with it. We should ask of the artist only that he give us a new experience, by permitting us to draw upon his resources of sensibility and power.

It would be very helpful at the outset to rule out the word "understand," which is so constantly used in connection with Modern Art, and substitute "experience." There is no need to strain after an intellectual understanding of paintings; indeed it is usually futile. Pictures are not made to be read like books. As Picasso has said, we do not ask to understand the song of a bird.

If you hear people say, "What is it?" when looking at a painting, you know they are searching for a literal image which will reassure them that they are in the presence of a work of art after all. How much more fruitful it would be if they said, "There it is!" and actually looked at the painting. It cannot be too strongly emphasized that paintings are visual experiences. One pamphlet on art appreciation devoted two pages to a detailed interpretation of a painting by Miro, only to conclude by warning the reader that other interpretations were possible. What nonsense! All one has to do in front of a Miro is to surrender oneself to a scene as gay, seductive and exciting as a circus. If you want to go on to decipher its symbolism later, fine! But first enjoy it.

When one comes face to face with the work of art in a receptive mood, there should be some kind of instantaneous recognition. There is danger here, because this recognition may be of a superficial kind; but I believe it must be present. Certainly one can go on to have a deeper experience after further acquaintance with the painting, but the first sensation is necessary to a critical appraisal. Perhaps one should only be guided by it after considerable experience.

Some people would make stronger reservations and perhaps even warn against first impressions. I believe, however, that it is only by cultivating the faculty of recognition that progress can be made. Art appreciation is not a cold-blooded intellectual exercise; it requires some of that *enivrement* that Baudelaire recommended as a normal state in human life. Don't be afraid to trust your own reactions, but don't be dogmatic. Be prepared to make so-called "mistakes"; they are the markers on any road to progress.

Standards of Criticism

We must from the beginning bring into play and develop our critical faculties. A great deal of what we look at will be superficial, mediocre, meaningless or tricky. Critical faculties can only be developed by educating the eye, as the ear must be trained to appreciate music. This involves long and loving attention to painting. Reading art books will help fill in the background, but there is no substitute for looking.

We have to assume that a work of art has intrinsic value, which will be discovered wholly, in part, or not at all, according to the perceptiveness of the viewer. Otherwise we would have to postulate the theory that the value of a work of art is relative to that found in it by the person who happens to be looking at it (Beauty is in the eye of the beholder) a proposition which can easily be reduced to absurdity. At any rate, anyone interested in art should try to discover value which exists and, by training his eye, find it in more refined forms than he has been capable of before.

It may be helpful at first to accept the consensus of informed opinion and study the works of artists who have achieved recognition. It may be argued that art critics have in the past been quite conspicuously unsuccessful in their appraisal of contemporary talent. It must be remembered that public art criticism, which began in the eighteenth century, was conducted by amateurs. Even such professional literary men as Ruskin and Baudelaire were amateurs of painting; nevertheless, they upheld Turner and Delacroix against public opinion.

Today a very large number of disinterested people (museum officials, art critics and collectors) are constantly scanning the contemporary scene, and it is safe to say that there are no undiscovered geniuses. Indeed there is a danger that young artists may be discovered too soon and be forced to don the uniform of success, which may prove constricting, before they have had time to adventure freely. However, I do not believe that a genuinely creative talent can be spoiled, even by success.

This acceptance of professional opinion need only be used as a help towards forming standards. The purpose of training our critical faculties is not to make negative or superior judgements, but to involve ourselves in the work.

This applies equally to our response to the art of the past, which is generally thought to be much easier to judge than Modern Art; indeed many people hold that values have ceased to exist. This is not true; in fact an artist in the non-objective field shows his stature to the trained eye as readily as does an artist in the objective field. Of course, it is easy for anyone to say, "The left arm is too long for the right," but this is a physiological judgement, not an aesthetic one. By these standards we would have to reject all the work of El Greco.

As we have already seen, the Old Masters did not have naturalism as a prime objective: they used formal means to expressive ends. To recognize and appreciate these means, one must have a trained eye. Without the training gained by appreciative looking, the average person will always prefer the work of an academician such as Augustus Egg to that of Turner.

Exactly the same standards must be brought to the consideration of a non-objective work as to an objective work—form and expressiveness. It does not take long for a normally sensitive person to learn to distinguish between the meaningless manipulation of paint and genuine expressiveness. There is an authority in a work of quality that makes itself felt even to those who do not fully understand its purpose.

Because art has become so individual, we must be prepared to find the work of some artists more sympathetic to us than that of others but this is not a basis for judgement. For instance, we may not like Mexican art of the Revolutionary period but we can still recognize its power and sincerity. We shall form similar preferences among the non-objective painters.

The Last Analysis

There are those who hold that you either "dig" or you don't. But that is dismissing the problem too easily: we must ask what it is that we seek in a work of art. A painting is a creation in pigment with its various colours and textures, and it is primarily through our eyes that appreciation and enjoyment must come. A pneumatic nude by Bronzino or a languorous slave by Alma Tadema cannot move us as can the palpable flesh of a Titian or a Renoir nude, not because of the way their parts are put together, but because of the way they are painted.

In Rembrandt's "A Woman Bathing" the whole of the forearm and wrist and part of the right hand are realized in one brush stroke, and the extraordinary vitality of this gesture produces in us a response to the intensity of the artist's vision. Velasquez, Goya, Fragonard and other great painters have given us this same sensuous enjoyment of the handling of paint, and so can the modern artist. It is virtuosity (or what Reynolds called facility) that we are talking about; but what is wrong with virtuosity, as long as it is not employed for its own sake?

Nor is "painterliness" the whole of it. We can be just as transported by the meticulously finished drawings of Ingres, not because they are so lifelike, but because the hard point has moved over the paper like the hand of God. The same inevitability can be found in a drawing by Matisse. In other words what we are witnessing in a work of art is a performance.

Technique and what the French call *matière* (the materials of painting) must serve the need of the work, but they are there for us to see, appraise and appreciate in every painting we look at. There are some modern artists who, in distrust of these very qualities, have scorned to use them; and they have done so successfully when the very crudity of their method contributes to the peculiar truth, power or expressiveness of their work. Dubuffet has written of his own method, ". . . this brutal manifestation in the picture of the material means used by the painter to sustain the objects represented, and which would seem to prevent them from in fact taking form, actually function for me in the opposite sense. It seems to me paradoxically to give the objects a stronger presence, or even, to be more accurate, renders such a presence more powerful, more impressive, more astonishing." Which brings us back to what we said earlier: everything must be subordinated to the good of the work. In a recent reaction against painterliness, some artists have dispensed with texture altogether and applied their colour in thin washes, often on unsized canvases.

So much for the means; now the painting itself. At the beginning of this essay we referred to paintings as communications, and it is what they communicate to us through our eyes that we have to weigh. The "form" of the work—that total organization of colour, line and mass in space—is the vehicle of the content. Art criticism has not found a vocabulary to describe painting and probably never will. Words such as "significant" and "meaningful" soon become so blurred by usage that we shudder to use them. As originally used, these words attempted to express the idea that a successful work of art should reveal itself to us as a complete and authentic statement, having some feeling of inevitability and authority, and as a unique experience. Walt Whitman, interpreting his own work, *Leaves of Grass,* mentions "the idea of Totality, of the All-successful, final certainties of each individual man, as well as the world he inhabits." We have already suggested that on first seeing a painting we should feel some immediate recognition. As Sir Herbert Read expressed it, "An artist works toward a unity that emerges progressively from his perception and manipulation of material quantities, whereas we who appreciate the result begin with this unity and afterward become aware of the isolated quantities which have cohered to produce it."

Whatever moves us does so because of the artist's expressive use of form. Compare, for example, a Victorian painting of beggar children, squatting on wet pavements in the warm lights of a theatre entrance, watching an elegant couple descending from a hansom cab, with Picasso's etching, "The Frugal Repast." In both cases we may feel pity, but in the first instance it is produced solely by the story-telling reference of the subject matter; in the latter it is induced by the lean incisive quality of the line, the expressive distortions, the depth of the artist's feelings, the "biting edge of truth." Our responses are different: in one case remote and somewhat sentimental, in the other involved, not only with the man and woman at their meal, but with suffering generally. It is not the verisimilitude of a work that produces this deeper feeling but its rectitude. For a further example, compare the Napoleonic battle scenes of Baron Gros with the "Disasters of War" by Goya. We have to recognize this same integrity, authenticity and uniqueness in contemporary art.

And now we have arrived at the point where we must discuss non-objective art specifically, because I know by experience that this is a real problem. Many people can go a long way to meet the abstract painter; as long as some recognizable element is left to reassure them they will follow, but once the thread is broken and they find themselves before a non-objective work they are lost and start thinking nervously about chimpanzees. It is a pity, because the division between objective and non-objective painting is not real: it certainly has no meaning for the creative artist. If he feels the need to use figurative elements he will do so; if he does not feel the need, he will omit them.

The first non-objective paintings were done by Kandinsky in 1910 and proceeded inevitably from his expressionist landscapes. This kind of painting is then only fifty years old and at the very beginnings of its development, yet people can always be found who are ready to bury it. "It's on its way out," they say. "There's a movement afoot back to realism." This is mostly wishful thinking. Personally I believe that because of its infinite possibilities non-objective art will continue to be developed side by side with objective art. (Recent developments in both objective and non-objective painting are shown in Part 2).

What then are the problems connected with non-objective art; and why do people feel they have to make excuses for it? One of the criticisms raised is that it is inhuman. It is frequently suggested that, in turning away from man's image, the artist has turned away from man himself. The question is, what is human? Surely a non-objective work which has engaged the whole of an artist's psyche must in some sense be human, even more so than some objective work which has engaged only his skill. Another objection is that, because the form is free, there may be other solutions possible besides that chosen by the artist. This is, of course, true, but other solutions would result in other paintings. If the artist has not convinced us by the solution he has found, the picture has not established its identity with us. The intuitive method of arriving at solutions is not confined to art; it is used wherever the creative mind is at work—even in mathematics and physics. There is no theoretical or logical argument to be maintained against non-objective art, which has already produced a large body of valuable work.

All non-objective paintings should be looked at as concrete objects that have been created by the artist, the content of which is embodied in the form. The range of form is from classic to romantic: from the exquisite modulations of Mondrian to the improvizations of the Action Painters. The range of content varies as much as the form: from Mondrian's attempt to reveal "the universal aspect of life" to the absorption of the Action Painters in the dynamism of the creative process. As we contemplate these paintings, they should reflect some aspect of our experience, as human beings, or extend that experience, and in this sense have significance for us. The experience in question may concern our perceptions or our emotions, or it may be transcendental. We can think of the paintings as vital plastic equivalents of the experience.

It is vain to try to translate all non-objective paintings into some aspect of reality. Science and metaphysics can no longer describe reality, so why should the artist confine himself to it? The painting itself is its own reality, and it is that with which we have to concern ourselves. The interpretation we put on it is not important.

This brings up the matter of titles, which seems to trouble some people. Titles may be records; they may be descriptive, suggestive of mood, or poetic, or they may have meaning for the artist only. They are interesting, sometimes informative, but not important; and people who concern themselves too much with them show that they are searching for literary rather than plastic values. After finishing a non-objective work an artist may look at it with some detachment and name it. We may give it a completely different interpretation without in any sense changing its existence, the only thing which matters.

Conclusion

In a great work of art something new and unique has been expressed. We shall come across few great works of art (the perspective of time is in any case needed for their full force to be felt) but we shall see many in which the elements of greatness can be discerned. Even a small talent perfectly expressed can give lasting pleasure.

Art is the employment of talent through the discipline of a medium. We have to set aside medium without talent (superficial art) and talent abused by overconcern with clever use of medium (gimmicky art).

What we should be looking for is a statement made by the artist with moral intent in an attempt to combine together formally an experience and a medium—no matter what his means or method.

Part Two

> "Too much to know,
> is to know naught but fame;
> And every godfather
> can give a name."

Love's Labour's Lost, Shakespeare

The naming or classification of works of art is a dangerous business indeed. To begin with, it is inexact and, worse, it tends to distract attention from the all-important work itself.

It is possible, for instance, to argue that all art may be divided into two major categories: classic and romantic. Yet we find an artist such as Ingres, whose work straddles both groups. He is classic in that his form represents an ideal concept; he is romantic in the very personal distortions which constitute that ideal. This classic-romantic polarity in art has sometimes been linked with the Apollonian and Dionysian concepts, the maxims of Apollo, "Nothing in excess" and "Know thyself," being set against the cult of Dionysus, a longing for the more instinctive and impulsive life, in which enthusiasm is valued more than prudence.

With this warning we will try to indicate the scope of contemporary art and suggest some of the sources of its immense diversity, using Canadian paintings to illuminate the text. The size of the volume limits the number of illustrations and, therefore, the artists whose work can be shown. We would have liked to use many more, but the purpose of the book is not to survey Canadian art. One other reservation; specific works have been selected which happen to be known to me and which seemed to serve best in the context in which they are used. They must not be considered to typify the work of each artist. In some cases the artist no longer paints in the manner illustrated here; where works are not recent, dates of the paintings are given. Also, the analysis is not chronological—all the kinds of painting shown here can be seen today—although most recent developments are specifically called "new." Headings are not capitalized to emphasize that the terms are not necessarily in general usage.

Objective Art

Here used to classify all paintings in which recognizable subject matter has been retained.

post-Impressionism As we have seen, Impressionism, with its limited objectives, soon came to an end as a creative movement. But man's lyrical joy before nature can never end, and the artist has found new ways to express it. (*See plate 1*)

expressionism Paintings of this group can best be recognized if we consider them as being expressive, that is to say possessing a strong personal point of view, conveyed by the manipulation of forms and, often, by the use of intense colour. El Greco's distortions are expressionist, so is Grunewald's powerful alterpiece at Eisenheim. The German Expressionists before the First World War distorted forms and used violent and completely arbitrary colour derived from the Fauves. Elements of expressionism pervade all Western art of the past, particularly in the north, and will undoubtedly always remain as a valid and vital characteristic of objective painting. (*See plates 2, 3*)

post-Cubism By this term we mean all art in which subject matter is distorted, dissected, rearranged for the purpose of the organization of the picture, which nevertheless retains the objective elements on which it was based. The prime progenitor of this group is Cubism, the first movement to explore the very vitals of picture making. Within its scope can be included the legion of artists who have remade the world after their own vision. (*See plate 4*)

realism Realism has appeared whenever a purgative force was needed to clear away a style which had become too self-conscious. For example, Caravaggio and his followers reacting against mannerism in the sixteenth century; Courbet and Daumier in their revolt against the preciosity of the Salon painters; the so-called Ashcan School in the United States in their deliberate choice of "impolite" subject matter. Realism has sometimes had political implications, as in the case of Daumier, or the Social Realists of the Depression days. Because of this emotional involvement of the artist in his subject, realism has often employed expressionist techniques. (*See plates 5, 6*)

super-realism Super-realists employ the technique of the naturalists but go beyond them in intention. The earliest works of this kind aimed to deceive the eye by evoking the illusory existence of architectural elements on bare walls or by painting false balustrades encircling domed ceilings. In the seventeenth century the Dutch still-life painters with their drops of water or flies on the fruit invited the exploring hand and provided the same kind of gratifying deception as do the waxworks of Madame Tussaud.

A different element has entered into modern super-realism. The intention now is not to deceive the eye, but to focus the attention on a subject by naturalistic means so acutely that we are really forced to "see" it, instead of accepting it as part of the common scene. Looked at with such concentration, even the most ordinary object may take on overtones of feeling and memory. Nostalgia is a powerful emotion and in its poignancy close to love. We try to capture for ourselves some of the experience of past lives and nullify their non-existence by holding them in our own consciousness. Similarly we cling to the present paraphanalia and the landscape of our environment in an effort to intensify our experience and savour the passing moment. (*See plate 7*)

surrealism Surrealism as a self-conscious movement developed out of the anarchism of the Dadaists after the First World War. As suggested in the text, this movement of the twentieth century was given impetus by research into the sub-conscious, but its protagonists claimed a heritage going back to the grotesques of Leonardo da Vinci, the fantasies of Hieronimus Bosch, and the Disparates of Goya. They used images from dreams or the sub-conscious in order to evoke the irrational and the marvellous. Their technique was usually extremely naturalistic, although they also employed real objects in weird confrontation for collages or constructions. The intention was to extend the scope of human experience beyond the strictures of conventional perception and rendering. (*See plates 8, 9*)

metaphysical painting It is not intended to suggest that this is a category in which to group specific paintings but rather to draw attention to a motive that informs many modern objective works. In this kind of painting the artist searches for visual equivalents of abstract concepts—through metaphor, allegory, symbolism or fantasy. (*See plates 10, 11, 12*)

imagists A whole group of artists conjure figures as mysterious presences, commenting on the character and condition of man in a manner not explicit to an individual but general to humanity. (*See plates 13, 14*)

new realism The difficulty which objective artists now face is to create an image valid for our own time. Whatever style they employ, they are in danger of recalling earlier artistic experiences. Subject matter itself balks the objective painter because the media of photography, film and television have dealt with it so compellingly and usurped the artist's role as historian, social commentator and propagandist. What anti-war picture can rival the photographs of Belsen, or social commentary the T.V. image of race riots? It is perhaps for this reason that a group of artists has in recent years presented the object itself in works which seem destined to be called "Pop Art." They incorporate real things (coat hangers, toilet cabinets, refrigerators) or naturalistic representations of things (soup cans, pies, or the faces of film stars.) In some cases, to eradicate style completely, they have used mechanical means for painting, such as stencils.

Undoubtedly these artists question the values of our society (usually called materialistic) and perhaps, by closely examining the objects on which we have become so dependent, help us to detach ourselves from them. But, at the same time, one cannot but feel that a certain affection for these objects is implied. The critical inspection is for the most part conducted in high good humour and with wit.

In new realism the furniture of our world is explored, turned round, enlarged, repeated, to savour it more fully, to probe and underline its mystery. If this is a return to the image, it is to the image of man in his full corporeality, reflected in the things with which he has chosen to surround himself. (*See plates 15, 16*)

new objectives If the final group of works in this analysis of objective paintings is compared with the final group of non-objective paintings, it will be seen that the division between them is without significance— a salutory conclusion. (*See plates 17, 20*)

Non-Objective Art Traditionally called "Abstract Art".
This includes a vast group of works in which no recognizable subject matter is retained. Because non-objective art encompasses every conceivable kind of expression, its works are immensely diverse. They vary from the tender, lyrical and poetic to the most violent, epic and disturbed; from vibrations set up by colour and movement to figurations probing mysterious experiences on the edge of human consciousness. These pictures are very difficult to describe in words, but perhaps we can generalize about them.
a) Because they have no subject matter in the literal sense, their content is their form.
b) This form consists of a composition in terms of the artist's proper vocabulary—line, mass, colour, space, organized into a homogeneous expressive statement.

c) The works will seldom have specific meaning for us, but they should communicate; if they do not, then the chances are that the work in question is a meaningless manipulation of paint. By communicate, we mean convey to us a vital visual experience akin to that which is received aurally when we listen to music, which is also not explicit in meaning. This experience might be further defined as enjoyment; of the total form, of its expressiveness and of its sensuous content.

d) Some of these works have had a long period of gestation; the artist comes to apprehend them slowly. Others are accomplished intuitively (by immediate insight.)

His past experience with form may lead the artist to do a long series of closely related paintings, which will continue until he has exhausted the theme, or until a fresh personal experience demands a new form of expression.

abstract impressionism Non-objective paintings that appear to be derived from visual data directly perceived and momentarily captured in light can be classed in this group. (*See plate 21*)

abstract expressionism This title may eventually be used to denote painting of the late 1940's and 1950's, particularly in the United States of America. For our purpose here we will use it to describe non-objective paintings of an expressionistic kind— that is, conveying very strong personal involvement by the artist himself and stemming from his own inner experience.

The form of the work is directed at a sub-conscious level. As the suggestions come to him the artist accepts, rejects or amends, using his intelligence, his past experience with form, his visual sensibility, his sensuous reaction to his materials—in fact, his whole artistic personality. Redon said, "Nothing in art is achieved by the will alone. Everything is done docilely submitting to the arrival of the 'unconscious.' The analytical spirit must be quick when it appears, but it afterwards is of little importance to remember it, as with each work it proposes a different problem to us."

Many of these paintings have been called "Action Paintings," a title proposed by the American critic, Harold Rosenberg, suggesting that the artist has performed a new and original act in time, which, unlike the act of the dancer or the improvising musician, remains for us to see and experience.

In these works the artist, in the act of painting, works with his medium towards a result charged with struggle, accident, inspiration and decision. He is always totally involved and finally in command. We can only judge a painting of this kind by the authority and integrity of the resulting communication. It may evoke any emotion; it may suggest any experience metaphorically. It may gather us into a visionary state in which we cannot accurately define our feelings but only know a sense of mystery, in which analogies escape us even as we try to seize them. Or it may present a visual adventure, inviting the eye to wander and find constant delights, without ever compassing the whole, so that the painting has a new experience for us each time we come back to it. (*See plates 18, 24*)

Because of their sub-conscious derivation, many abstract expressionist paintings are submerged surrealist works; instead of defining dream content exactly, they suggest dream states, weird landscapes, strange confrontations, unknowable experiences, like those felt on waking from a dream whose story cannot be recalled. (*See plates 19, 25*)

classical abstracts If we consider classical art as the antithesis of expressionist or romantic art, as an ideal arrived at through a conceptual rather than a perceptual process, then we would expect paintings in this category to be somewhat austere and withdrawn, their beauty stemming from a sensitivity to form of an architectural nature; in other words constructions in paint. This they are; but more. In his struggle to express his concept of space, the artist must also rely on intuitive powers to lend it vitality. (*See pages 22, 23, 26*)

abstract images I have invented this category for non-objective paintings which are too conceptual to be called abstract expressionist works and too figurative to be included with classical abstracts. (*See plate 28*)

new non-objectives For obvious reasons these paintings have been called "Hard Edge." They represent a reaction to the urgency of abstract expressionism. They are less tumultuous, more considered, more refined. For instance, they dispense with heavy textures and rely on a purely visual reaction. They are decorative like the late "Jazz" series of paper cut-outs by Matisse; the word "decorative" is often used in a derogatory sense—not here. Compare these paintings with those in the section "new objectives." (*See plates 27, 29, 30, 31, 32*)

The two most recent developments of non-objective painting have been called "post-painterly abstractions" and "op art." As usual these categories are inexact. The former relates to canvases (like that of Jack Bush) which are thinly painted, sometimes stained onto unsized canvas, and tend to be lyrical. The latter refers to paintings which rely for their effect on optical reactions, expressive of movement, vitality, and energy and are a further extension of classical geometric art. Both continue the reaction against abstract expressionism.

1 Landscape with River by John Korner.
Oil 50″ x 36″.
Collection: Mr. & Mrs. L. Lazonick.
In this picture Korner has moved far from Impressionism. Local colour has been modified to the extent that it is no longer possible to define exactly the bounds of land and water. Planes have been flattened and the organization of perspective is more oriental than western. Yet the limpid and luminous quality of Impressionism remains.

2 Dark Self, 1957, by Mashel Teitelbaum.
Oil 40″ x 30″.
Collection: The artist.
Artists usually dramatize their self-portraits. Teitelbaum does also in
this highly expressive work. The figure, disturbingly painted, is
crowned by a head of brooding compassion.

3 Late Afternoon, Georgian Bay by Goodridge Roberts.
Oil 32" x 48".
Collection: Mr. & Mrs. J. Ballantyne.
The use of strong colour and violent brushwork produces a sense of
vitality, ruggedness and deep personal involvement in the Georgian
Bay scene. It is a good example of the use of paint, not to reproduce
a landscape, but to convey the artist's feelings about it.

4 Black Table and Rubber Plant, 1948 by Jacques de Tonnancour.
Oil 33½" x 45".
Collection: The Art Gallery of Toronto.
The first thing we notice in this painting is that the laws of perspective
and gravity have been disregarded and all planes referred to the
picture surface. Depth is shallow as in Cubism. Sharpened edges
contrasted with full forms set up a rhythmic movement which both
enlivens the composition and unifies it.

5 243 Bleecker Street by Albert Franck.
Oil 10″ x 12″.
Collection: Mr. & Mrs. F. M. Gaby.
If realism is the opposite of the ideal, we have it in this painting of
old Toronto houses. Sharp tonal contrasts effectively set the bleak
mood of a winter's day.

6 Variation on a Theme by Poussin by Philip Surrey.
  Oil 16″ x 24″.
  Collection: The Art Gallery of Hamilton.
  It is interesting that Surrey has based his composition on a painting
  by one of history's most classical artists; but the violence of the
  movement and the distortion of forms are expressionistic and the
  earthy subject matter of a car crash is realistic.

7 The Bicycle by Hugh MacKenzie.
  Tempera 24″ x 26″.
  Collection: Mr. & Mrs. C. R. B. Salter.
  We are concerned with the passing moment here. The girl's hand
  on the bicycle wheel has just stopped its turning. It will turn again and
  she will ride away, but her whole life seems concentrated in this
  exact instant in which she looks out at the distant landscape.

8 Horse and Train by Alex Colville.
Tempera 16" x 21¼".
Collection: The Art Gallery of Hamilton.
The dreamlike quality of this painting is obvious. The horse and
train seem to be moving towards some final fated meeting.

9 The Oakdales Reunion by Tony Urquhart.
Oil collage 28″ x 44″.
Collection: The Art Gallery of Toronto.
The surrealist element in this work is the incongruity of the figures
in football garb seated in a grove of trees. We know that time has
elapsed since their "photos" were taken—they may now be prosperous
business men; they may even be dead. We know nothing of their
story, only that they played football together, but the picture invites
speculation on how they lived their lives and, hence, how we have
lived ours.

10 Presences after Fire, 1950, by J. L. Shadbolt.
   Casein 26¼″ x 36¼″.
   Collection: The National Gallery of Canada.
   In these mask-like figures and effigies the artist seems to be
   commenting on the variety, vitality and indestructibility of life,
   including human life.

11 Family Group by Louis de Niverville.
  Oil 48″ x 72″.
  Collection: Mr. & Mrs. Percy Waxer.
  This is a fantastic rendering of a family, deliberately enhanced by the
  use of a primitive style. Possibly de Niverville is drawing on memories
  of his own youth. In any case these very real presences constitute
  a whimsical concept of the idea of family.

12 L'Ange Blanc by Jean-Paul Lemieux.
   Oil 50¼″ x 22¾″.
   Collection: Mr. & Mrs. R. A. Hutchison.
   One is tempted to see here an allegoric reference to the narrative of
   the Angel of the Annunciation. Lemieux's angel is on earth and the
   features remind us, not of a heavenly visitor but of the many
   Québécois he has painted.

13 Myth #2, The River by Graham Coughtry.
   Oil 60″ x 60″.
   Collection: Dr. & Mrs. S. Wax.
   Coughtry has for some years evoked presences from the
   circumfusion of paint and in the series to which this painting belongs
   he has sought a symbolic human archetype in the myth of
   Hermaphroditus, who became one with the nymph Salmacis.

14 The Judges by Shizueye Takashima.
   Oil 41″ x 36″.
   Collection: The artist.
   Takashima preserves the anonymity of her figures by concealing
   their features. Imagists often present human beings as victims. Here are
   their judges, and in the force of this painting justice itself is called
   into question.

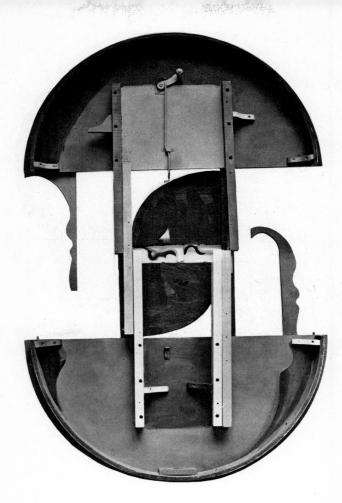

15 Homage to the French Revolution by Gordon Rayner.
Painted construction 70″ x 46″.
Collection: The Art Gallery of Toronto.
The object used in this case is a table, seen from underneath, which,
with its extension mechanism, suggests a guillotine. By adding to this
familiar object and painting it red, white and blue, Rayner has given
it the force of "personality" in its own right and nudged our memory
of a dramatic event in the history of the Western world.

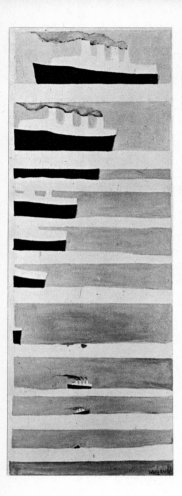

16 Tragedy at Sea by Joyce Wieland.
   Oil 50″ x 18″.
   Collection: Mr. & Mrs. V. Svarre.
   Pop elements in this picture are two-fold. First the use of the film-
   strip technique with its implied staccato motion, and secondly the
   introduction of a familiar glamorous object, the great liner with all
   the folklore attaching to it. Incidentally, the painting in blue, black and
   white is very satisfying in completely abstract terms.

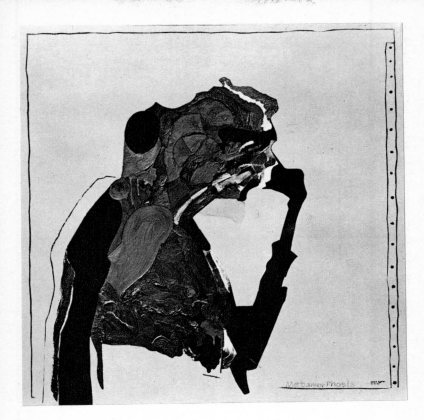

17 Metamorphosis by Dennis Burton.
   Oil 39½″ x 39½″.
   Collection: The Isaacs Gallery.
   This painting is figurative (which the artist acknowledges in the title)
   but I suspect that this was not his intention when he started it. The
   seventeenth century artist Arcimboldo built up grotesque heads with
   vegetables; Burton does it with flat areas of colour, partly geometric,
   and probably accepted and developed the figure as it appeared.

18 Victoire by Rita Letendre.
   Oil 82″ x 108″.
   Collection: Mr. and Mrs. P. Waxer.
   The expressive qualities of this painting are evident. It relies for its
   effect on vigorous brushwork and movement, the resonant flamelike
   reds seeming to devour the central black and white forms.
   Compare with the Roberts landscape.

19 Puritan Place by Harold Town, (1960).
   Oil 80″ x 80″.
   Collection: The artist.
   We should bear in mind that Town has gone about this painting
   without conscious intent. We read it as both a place and an event—an
   event because the variously paced movements convey the idea of
   a happening: the swift stabs of the jagged whites, the slow sinister
   progress of the orange shapes from the right, the flamelike flicker of the
   centre ground contained by the red diamond, and the poise before
   movement of the threatening figure at top left. There is no need to
   carry analysis further to realize that this dream landscape, which is
   still immensely believable, is an excellent example of the contribution
   made by surrealism to abstract expressionism.

20 Black and White (Walking Woman) by Michael Snow.
Enamels on canvas 61″ x 66″.
Collection: The Isaacs Gallery.
In his long series of "cut-out" women, Snow has set himself problems
that are fundamentally pictorial. Yet when we look at the
paintings and explore their ambiguous space, the woman is there—
"a conventional sign," to quote the dictionary definition of a symbol,
"of some object or idea or process"—evocative, yet indivisible from
the space problem.

21 Crete 1959 by Robert Hedrick.
   Oil 48″ x 84″.
   Collection: Mrs. Dorothy Cameron Moes.
   This is one of a series of paintings by Hedrick that one might think of
   in relation to grasses or growing vegetation moving in light.
   Actually it is a highly organized work, fugue-like in formality.
   Nevertheless the natural visual reference of this series allows us to
   classify them as impressionistic. Compare with the painting by
   John Korner.

22 Core Structure by Kazuo Nakamura.
Oil 36½" x 42".
Collection: The artist.
Nakamura deals with both microcosm and macrocosm. Though
many of his paintings refer to inner structure they can be read equally
in terms of landscape. This painting resembles some of his lake
landscapes, with their high horizon and descending planes contained by
foreground elements. These paintings breathe with subtle life and in
their great restraint provide constant refreshment.

23 Simultanéité by Guido Molinari.
Oil 56" x 48".
Collection: The artist.
Paintings of this kind are often called "Geometric Art" because they
are architecturally organized from the simplest shapes. The dynamics
of vision are used to make colours react against each other and
continuously change as the eye picks up the various bands and
transposes them on adjoining areas. In Molinari's picture the
preponderance of dark tones at the edges concentrates attention to the

centre where the red stripes recede and become the ground, thus setting
up a sense of space.
Successful paintings of this kind convey a state of tension in suspense.
Some of them, by employing large areas of saturated colour,
suggest fields of force and involve the looker physically in what we
might call a post-Berenson tactile experience.

24 Painting for John Cage by Charles Gagnon.
Oil 58″ x 52″.
Collection: The artist.
Even in black and white reproduction the epic quality of this
painting is apparent. One seems to be witness to an event of such
immediacy that it makes the battles, brigands, stormy skies and horrific
gorges of the romantic age pale to harmless stage plays. The question
of time is interesting in connection with abstract expressionism.
In a bandit or shipwreck picture by Salvator Rosa (seventeenth
century), for instance, one can consider the story in terms of before and
after, but Gagnon's painting has no past or future, only a present.
Note how the much scorned "drips" set up directions of movement.

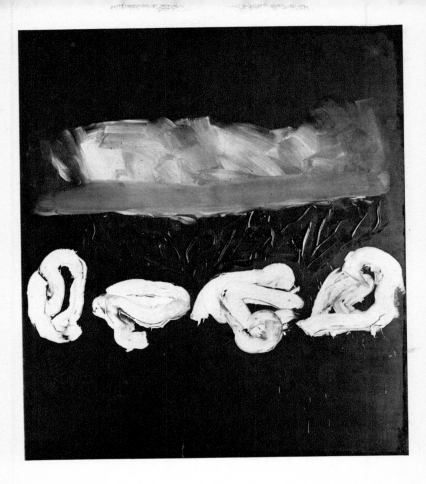

25 Day of Judgement by Richard Gorman.
   Oil 86″ x 72″.
   Collection: Mr. and Mrs. Charles S. Band.
   Whether or not Gorman began this painting with the subject in
   mind is not important; he probably did not. What matters is that,
   using the procedures of abstract expressionism, he has produced a
   powerful image with both figurative and surrealist connotations.

26 Le Drapeau inconnu by Jean Albert McEwen.
Oil 80″ x 75″.
Collection: Mr. and Mrs. R. Bennett.
This painting is included with the classical group because it is
obviously constructed as a series of planes in depth. These planes are
themselves developed by interpenetrating layers of colour which react
against each other to make a vibrant textural surface. It comes close
to being expressionist in effect.

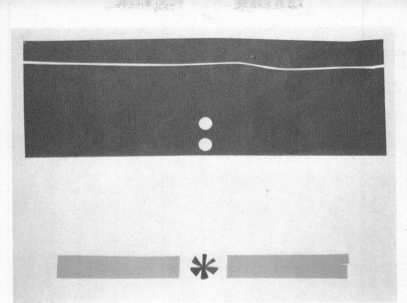

27 Snow by William Ronald.
   Oil 60″ x 80″.
   Collection: Kootz Gallery.
   The decorative quality of this painting is evident, yet, despite the
   extreme economy of means, it remains expressive. It is hard to know
   whether the word "snow" would have come to mind without the title,
   but the painting may well reflect a memory of Ronald's Canadian
   childhood. Although the painting is dead flat, the white line bisecting
   the blue area suggests a horizon and the white balls seem to fall towards
   the turning star-like form below (snow balls, snow flake?)
   Anyway, the cold blues add purity to the large white area, giving
   the picture a kind of austere, yet light, beauty.

28 Alchimie, 1960 by Alfred Pellan.
  Oil 14⅜" x 11".
  Collection: Mr. and Mrs. Walter Stewart.
  On first looking at this picture one becomes conscious of an image
  both evolving and mechanical. Closer inspection reveals this image
  to be a coalescence of signs expressing an alchemy of organic and
  mechanical forms. It could also be called metaphysical, surrealist or
  symbolic, and illustrates the point made by Mathieu that a sign
  may itself become viable.

29 Byzantium by Ronald Bloore (1961).
Oil 48″ x 48″.
Collection: Mr. & Mrs. Michael Taylor.
There is more movement in this painting than in the Ronald; the
hard-edge shapes circle the cross in an outward whirl which throws
them finally off the canvas. There is no need to try to read meaning
into paintings of this kind (as we did in the previous example); though
titles give rise to speculation, they are always afterthoughts. Bloore's
picture should be accepted for what it is—a concrete and lively object
which, with its orange ground, seems to carry some implications of
glory and invites contemplation.

30 Green Garden by Jack Bush.
   Oil 46″ x 80″.
   Collection: The artist.
   In 1961 Bush produced a series of highly lyrical paintings. His
   intention, he says, was to paint the most beautiful pictures he could, to
   make them sing. He succeeds here in a painting where the unfolding
   organic form to the left is contrasted with the white thrust from the
   right, both in an aura of green. Beneath its deceptive simplicity lies
   a deeply felt poetic quality, clearly related to nature.

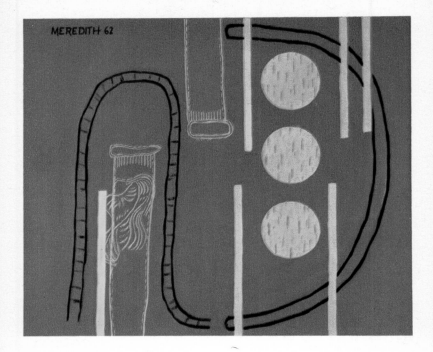

31 Samurai (1962) by John Meredith.
   Oil 42″ x 50″.
   Collection: The Isaacs Gallery.
   Like the others of this group, this strange picture is thinly painted,
   but it is more graphic. The regal colour and the oriental quality of
   some of the drawing may have suggested the title. It seems to be on the
   point of telling some story, the black curved lines hinting at a child's
   depiction of a journey.

32 Avenir 1961 by Marcel Barbeau.
   Oil 72″ x 55″.
   Collection: Galerie du Siècle.
   During his last years in Paris Borduas increasingly refined his work
   until nothing was left but the *silence magnétique* of his final black and
   white paintings. Barbeau seems to have taken up where Borduas
   left off, dispensing even with texture in his black and white series. The
   subject of this painting is simply space and if we are not engulfed in
   this great white area which is given definition by the bounding black
   edge, then the picture fails us. What is lost in reproduction is scale.